IT'S A FACT! Real-Life Reads

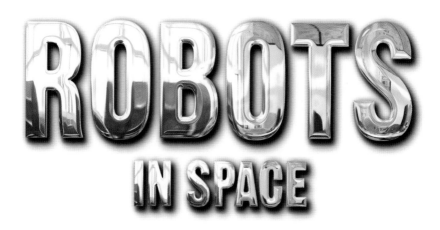

ROBOTS IN SPACE

by Ruth Owen

Consultants:

Suzy Gazlay, MA
Recipient, Presidential Award for Excellence in Science Teaching

Kevin Yates
Fellow of the Royal Astronomical Society

Ruby Tuesday Books

Published in 2015 by Ruby Tuesday Books Ltd.

Editor: Mark J. Sachner
Designer: Emma Randall
Production: John Lingham

Photo Credits:
ESA–A. Le Floc'h: 29 (top); ESA: 29 (bottom); NASA: Cover, 4–5, 7
(bottom), 8–9, 10–11, 12–13, 14–15, 16–17, 18–19, 20–21, 22–23, 25,
27, 28 (Matt Deans), 31; NOAA: 6; Thermite by Howe and Howe
Technologies: 7 (top).

Library of Congress Control Number: 2013920125

ISBN 978-1-909673-48-9

Printed and published in the United States of America

For further information including rights and permissions requests, please
contact our Customer Service Department at 877-337-8577.

CONTENTS

Life on Mars

The Sun is rising. It's morning on Mars. Millions of miles from Earth, a hardworking member of **NASA**'s team begins its day.

The temperature is colder than the North Pole in December. Fierce winds are blowing. The air is made up of poisonous gases. These dangers do not harm the busy worker, though. That's because it is a **robot**.

Even a robot can take selfies! *Curiosity* sends photos of itself back to Earth. This allows the scientists who control *Curiosity* to make sure it's in good shape.

What is a Robot?

A robot is a machine that can do jobs. Often a robot does work that is too dangerous for a person to do.

Some robots explore shipwrecks, while others fight fires. In space, robots can repair spacecraft, explore, and even do experiments.

Inside a robot, there is a computer that acts a little like a brain. A person uploads instructions to the robot's computer brain. Then the robot carries out the instructions. Once they have their instructions, some robots can work on their own for days, months, or even years. Other robots need a human operator to control every move they make.

Hercules

The wreck of the RMS Titanic

Hercules is a robot that can explore shipwrecks. It takes photos and makes videos. It can do this work up to 2.5 miles (4 km) under the ocean.

The robot's name is *Curiosity*, and its job is to study Mars. It would be very dangerous for a human scientist to do this work. For a robot, however, working in this extreme place is not a problem.

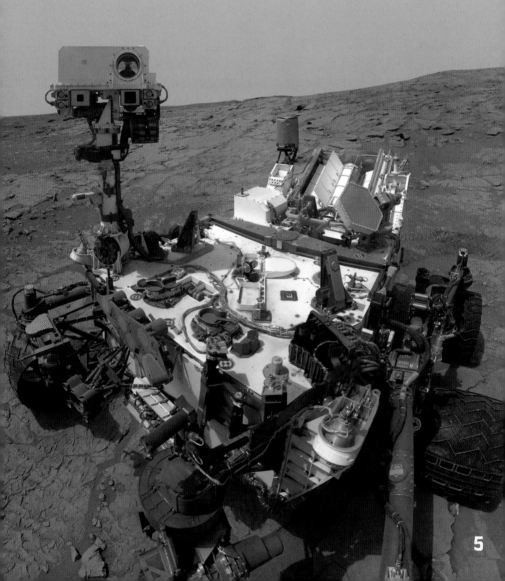

This robot fights fires that are too dangerous for a human firefighter to approach.

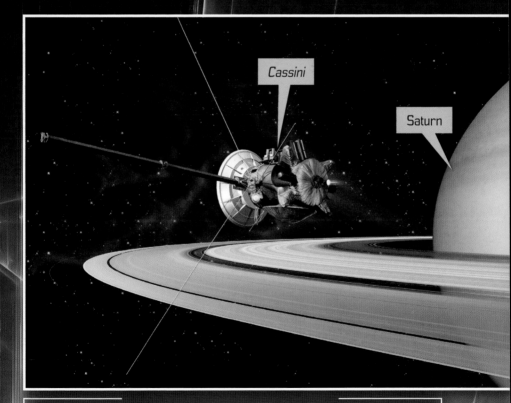

Cassini

Saturn

This illustration shows the space probe *Cassini*. This robot is studying Saturn.

A Mission to Mars

Curiosity is a type of robot known as a **rover**. A rover is a robot that has wheels. It is able to move from place to place.

Curiosity is the fourth rover to explore the surface of Mars. The earlier rovers are named *Sojourner*, *Spirit*, and *Opportunity*. *Curiosity* was sent to Mars to discover if there was once water on the planet. If there was water, tiny living things called **microbes** may have lived on Mars. To find signs of life on another planet would be a huge discovery!

Curiosity's **mission** began on November 26, 2011. Safely packed inside a spacecraft, it blasted off from Earth aboard a rocket. The illustrations on these pages show *Curiosity's* journey to Mars.

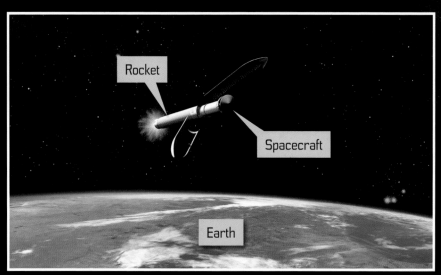

Rocket

Spacecraft

Earth

Once the rocket was in space, *Curiosity's* spacecraft separated from the rocket.

After more than eight months, the spacecraft reached Mars. At high speed, it hurtled toward the planet.

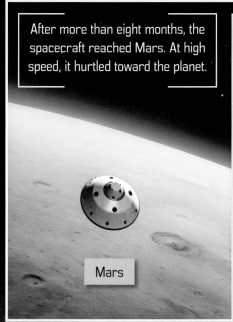

Mars

Parachute

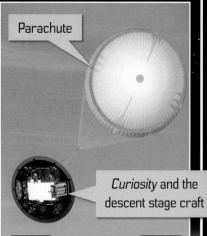

Curiosity and the descent stage craft

A parachute opened to slow the spacecraft. The bottom of the spacecraft popped off to reveal *Curiosity* and the descent stage craft.

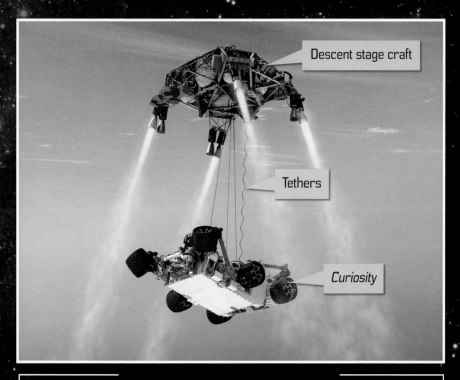

Descent stage craft

Tethers

Curiosity

Finally, the descent stage left the spacecraft. It carefully lowered *Curiosity* to the ground on tethers. Then the descent stage flew away and crash landed.

A Robot at Work

Curiosity landed on Mars on August 6, 2012.
It soon got to work studying the surface
of the planet.

Curiosity sends photos and movies of Mars back
to Earth. Then human scientists can examine them.
It looks for clues that streams once flowed on Mars.

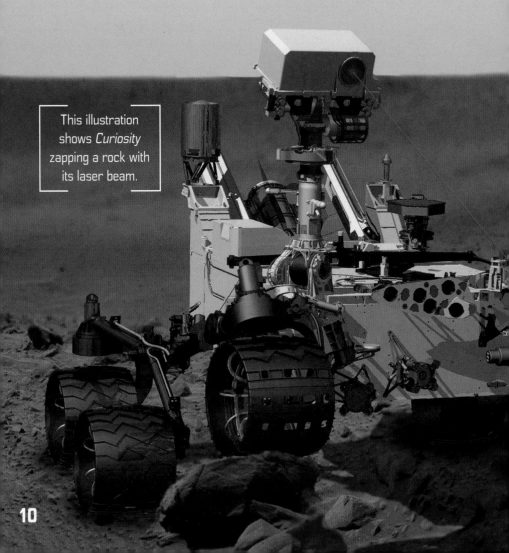

This illustration
shows *Curiosity*
zapping a rock with
its laser beam.

The robot also examines rocks and soil to find out what **chemicals** they contain. It uses a laser beam to zap rocks. As the rock heats up, it gives off gases. The robot investigates the gases to discover what the rock is made of. *Curiosity* also drills holes in the ground to loosen soil. It does this with a drill on its long arm. Then it scoops up the soil and tests it. Certain chemicals in rocks and soil can be a clue that microbes once lived on Mars.

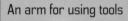

An arm for using tools

Curiosity's Stats

Length: 10 feet (3 m)

Width: 9 feet (2.7 m)

Height: 7 feet (2.1 m)

Weight: 2,000 pounds (907 kg)

Length of arm: 7 feet (2.1 m)

Top speed: 100 feet (30 m) an hour

Number of cameras aboard: 17

Controlling a Robot

Hundreds of scientists and **engineers** worked as a team to build *Curiosity* and send it to Mars.

Today, a team of NASA scientists controls the robot from Earth. When night falls on Mars, *Curiosity* stops work. *Curiosity's* controllers then spend the Martian night planning the next day. They plan every inch of the route that *Curiosity* will travel. They also plan every task that the robot will do. As morning comes, the controllers upload the instructions to *Curiosity*. Then they tell it to wake up and start work.

Curiosity's computer brain can also think for itself. Using its cameras, the robot keeps watch for unexpected dangers. This stops it from crashing into a large rock or falling off a cliff!

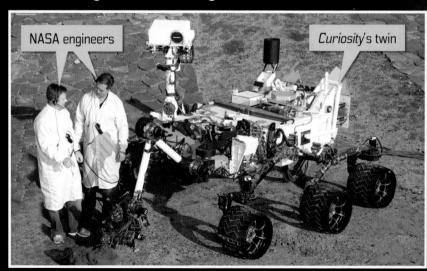

NASA engineers

Curiosity's twin

Sometimes scientists try out a task on Earth before asking *Curiosity* to do it. They do this using a robot that's a copy, or twin, of *Curiosity*.

Curiosity's Discoveries

Curiosity found an area of ground where a stream once flowed. This proves that billions of years ago, there was water on Mars.

Earth

Mars

The dried-up Mars stream looks similar to a dried-up stream on Earth.

Soil

Drill hole

Curiosity's scoop filled with Mars soil for testing

Curiosity drilled these holes on Mars. It studied the chemicals in the soil. The chemicals proved that Mars was once a place where living things could survive.

A Robotic Arm

Curiosity works millions of miles from Earth. Other space robots work closer to their home planet.

Canadarm2 is a large robotic arm that works on the International Space Station, or ISS. The space station is about 248 miles (400 km) above Earth's surface. Astronauts live and carry out science experiments aboard the space station.

Astronaut

Canadarm2 was fitted to the International Space Station in 2001. Sometimes, new sections of the ISS are delivered by spacecraft. Then the robot arm fits them in place. Sometimes, an astronaut must make repairs to the outside of the ISS. The astronaut can be moved into place by *Canadarm2*.

Canadarm2

An astronaut inside the space station controls *Canadarm2*. The astronaut uses joysticks to move the arm.

Canadarm2 is 57.7 feet (17.6 m) long. It has seven joints, or sections, that bend.

Space Station Robots

Canadarm2 is able to move around the outside of the International Space Station.

It does this by flipping end over end. It looks a little like a gymnast tumbling very slowly. The robot arm can also be attached to a trolley-like machine. Then it rolls along the outside of the ISS on tracks.

Dextre

In 2008, *Canadarm2* was joined by a robot named *Dextre*. The new robot arrived at the ISS aboard the space shuttle *Endeavour*.

Dextre's job is to make repairs on the space station. *Dextre* can be attached to the end of *Canadarm2*, like a hand. Then *Canadarm2* moves *Dextre* to where it's needed.

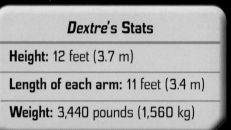

Dextre's Stats

Height: 12 feet (3.7 m)

Length of each arm: 11 feet (3.4 m)

Weight: 3,440 pounds (1,560 kg)

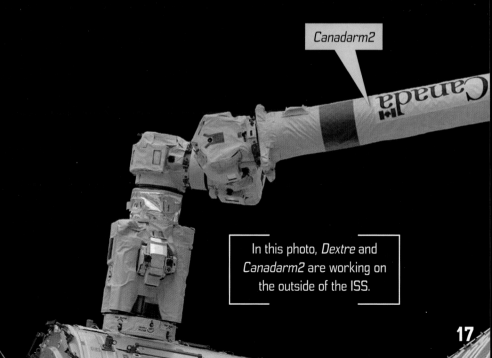

Canadarm2

In this photo, *Dextre* and *Canadarm2* are working on the outside of the ISS.

It's a Job for Dextre

When something needs fixing outside the space station, it's a job for *Dextre*.

Scientists from NASA and the Canadian Space Agency plan all *Dextre's* tasks. Then they upload instructions to the robot. *Dextre* can make repairs to electrical equipment. It can change batteries. It also replaces damaged cameras on the outside of the space station. *Dextre* even has its own tool kit. The tools can be fitted to the robot's arms, like fingers!

Dextre does many jobs that astronauts once had to do. This keeps astronauts from having to make dangerous **spacewalks**. Now astronauts can stay safe inside the space station. They also have more time to carry out important experiments.

This photo shows *Dextre* and *Canadarm2* in 2011. They are unloading supplies from the space shuttle *Discovery*. The space shuttle is docked with the space station.

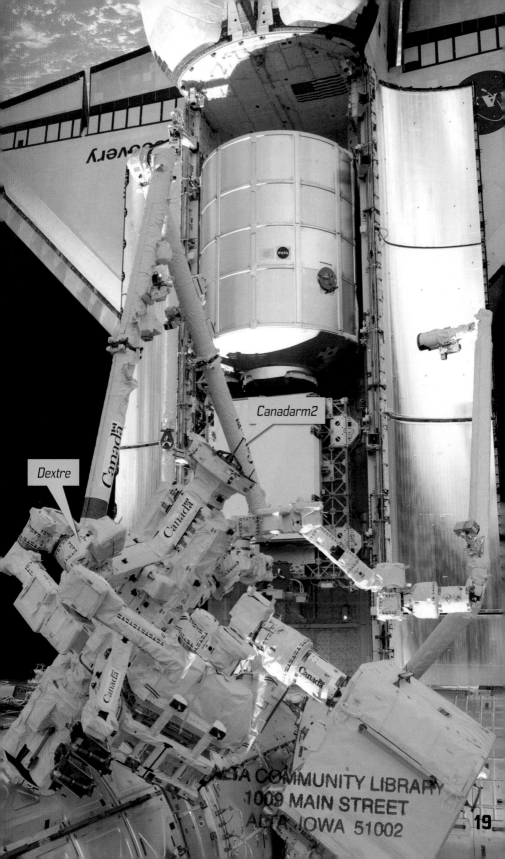

Dextre

Canadarm2

A Robot Astronaut

What do you name a robot that's an astronaut? You call it *Robonaut*, of course! *Robonaut* is a type of **humanoid** robot that will do work in space.

The computer inside *Robonaut* helps it think for itself. A controller gives the robot a task to do. Then the robot figures out how to do it. Cameras inside the robot's head allow it to see.

A *Robonaut* meets an astronaut!

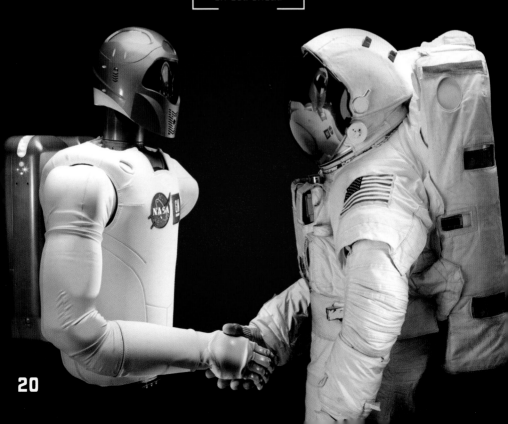

A *Robonaut* using a cell phone to tweet

Robonaut's hands work just like a human's hands. Its fingers can even do fiddly tasks such as using a cell phone.

A *Robonaut* on its wheeled base

Robonaut can be attached to a base with wheels. This would allow the robot to move around on the Moon or even another planet!

A Robonaut in Space

Engineers from NASA and General Motors have built four *Robonaut* robots. In 2011, one of the robots, named *Robonaut 2B*, went into space!

Robonaut 2B, or *R2B* for short, blasted off aboard the space shuttle *Discovery*. It traveled to the International Space Station.

R2B is the first humanoid robot in space. Its mission is to be a test robot. Scientists can give *R2B* tasks. Then they can learn how well it works in space.

R2B takes off for space as *Robonaut R2A* waves goodbye.

Robonaut's Future

In April 2014, *Robonaut 2B* received
a very special delivery from Earth.
A pair of legs arrived at the space
station aboard a spacecraft.

R2B's legs allow it to slowly move around
the space station. It has special toe-like parts
on the ends of its legs. These end parts can
attach to walls and ceilings.

In the future, humanoid robots may work
alongside astronauts. Because they are the
same shape as humans, they can work in
the same places. Their robot hands can do
the same jobs. They can even use tools and
machines made for humans.

Robots like *R2B* could do everyday tasks
such as checking equipment. They could also
do dangerous jobs, such as making repairs
outside of a spacecraft!

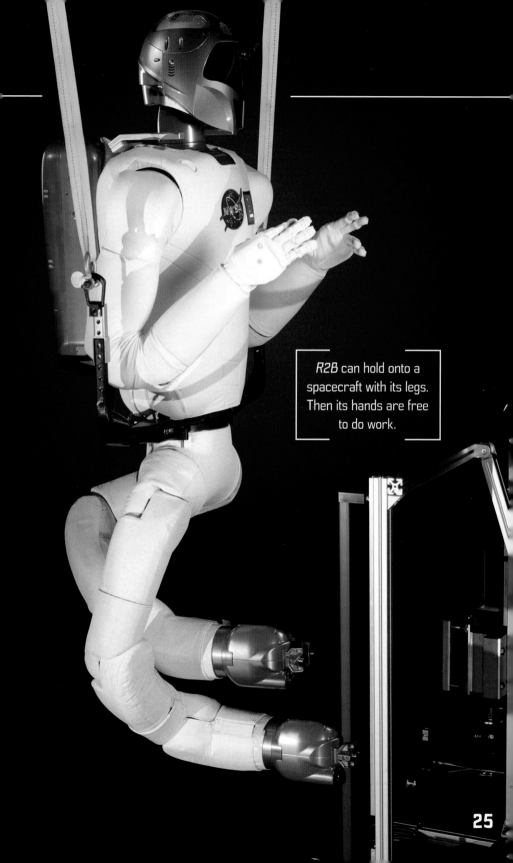

R2B can hold onto a spacecraft with its legs. Then its hands are free to do work.

Meet the SPHERES

Not all space robots have wheels, legs, or bodies.

Aboard the International Space Station are three robots called SPHERES. The robots' name is a code for a much longer official name. Each SPHERES robot is about the size of a bowling ball.

Inside the space station, the force of **gravity** is very weak. This means an object floats unless it is attached to a surface. The SPHERES float in the air. They move by using parts called thrusters. The thrusters gently whoosh them through the air.

SPHERES can move around as a group. They are able to sense each other and their surroundings. They don't bump into each other or other objects. If a SPHERES robot is knocked, it moves back to its original position. Scientists are doing experiments with the SPHERES. They want to find out what jobs the floating robots could do.

The three SPHERES are orange, red, and blue.

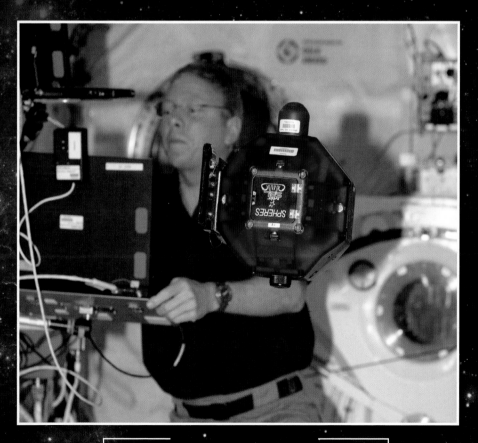

The red SPHERES robot takes part in an experiment.

Space Robots in the Future

All over the world, scientists and engineers are designing new robots.

NASA is working on robot explorers called *K10* robots. These robots could be sent to other planets or the Moon. The robots would explore and send information back to Earth. The information would help scientists plan missions for human astronauts.

Some scientists are working on new ways for people to control robots. A doctor on Earth could wear a robotic arm. This would control a robot's arm. The robot might be on a spacecraft, millions of miles from Earth. The doctor could make the robot operate on an injured astronaut.

Space is a dangerous place. With help from robots, however, humans can keep on exploring. The future for **robotics** is exciting!

A *K10* robot explorer

This scientist is working on a robotic suit called an exoskeleton.
The person wearing the suit can control a robot.

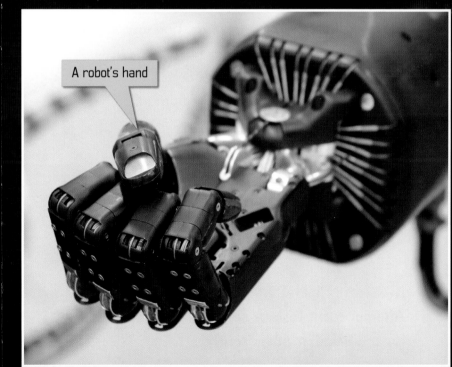

A robot's hand

Glossary

chemical (KEM-uh-kuhl)
A substance, or mixture of substances, found on Earth or in space. For example, hydrogen and nitrogen are both chemicals. Chemicals exist naturally. They can also be made by people.

engineer (en-juh-NIHR)
A person who uses math, science, and technology to design and build machines such as cars, spacecraft, or robots. Some engineers design and build structures such as skyscrapers or bridges.

gravity (GRAV-uh-tee)
The force that pulls things toward the center of Earth and keeps them from drifting into space.

humanoid (HYOO-muhn-oid)
Having the shape or look of a human.

microbe (MY-krobe)
A living thing that is so tiny it can only be seen with a microscope, not with a person's eyes alone. The germs that make people sick are types of microbes.

mission (MISH-uhn)
An important task or series of tasks carried out for a particular purpose.

NASA (NA-suh)
A group of scientists and space experts in the United States. NASA studies space and builds spacecraft. The letters in NASA stand for "National Aeronautics and Space Administration."

robot (ROH-bot)
A machine that is programmed by a computer to do work automatically. Robots often do jobs that people can do.

robotics (roh-BOT-ikss) The technology that is used to design and build robots.

rover (ROH-vur)
A robot with wheels that is used to explore a planet.

spacewalk (SPAYSS-wawk)
An activity in which an astronaut goes outside of a spacecraft or space station while in space. An astronaut might need to make a spacewalk to carry out repairs on a spacecraft.

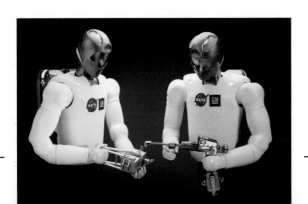

Index

Read More

Shulman, Mark, and James Buckley Jr. Robots (Time For Kids Explorers). New York: Time For Kids Books (2014).

Stewart, Melissa. Robots (National Geographic Readers). Washington, D.C.: National Geographic Children's Books (2014).

Learn More Online

To learn more about robots in space, go to
www.rubytuesdaybooks.com/robots